T0085455

ŠEVČÍK
Op. 8

CHANGES OF POSITION & PREPARATORY
SCALE STUDIES

LAGENWECHSEL UND TONLEITERVORSTUDIEN

CHANGEMENT DE POSITIONS ET
EXERCICES PRÉPARATOIRES DE GAMMES

for

VIOLA
(ALTO)

arranged / bearbeitet / arrangées

by   von   par

Lionel Tertis

Bosworth

REMEMBER!

(1) The first consideration in string playing, is the attainment of *perfect intonation*. This can only be achieved by the most *intense* and *concentrated* listening, (not superficial listening). *Never* pass a note that is the slightest degree out of tune.

(2) *Hold* and *keep* your fingers down on the strings in all these exercises, whenever and wherever it is at all possible.

(3) Attention must be paid to accurate note *values*. Be particularly careful when there are two notes with *separate* bows, immediately followed by two notes of the same value in one bow, or one note separately, followed by three notes of the same value in one bow etc. etc. No matter how varied the groupings, every note must be of exact equal value.

(4) When practising these exercises *slowly* lift your fingers high and feel you are doing so from the *knuckles* and bring your fingers down hard on the fingerboard,—when practising them *rapidly*, do not lift your fingers high and put them down *lightly* on the fingerboard.

(5) Divide the bowing up so as to, *first*, practise the exercises slowly and play them in tune. When you can do this efficiently, use the bowing as indicated, or as many notes in the one bow as possible.

NOTICE

(1) La première qualité qu'il faut s'appliquer à obtenir, lors de l'étude de tout instrument à cordes, est la *justesse d'intonation*. Celle-ci ne s'acquiert qu'au prix d'une attention *soutenue* et *concentrée* (pas d'attention superficielle). Veillez donc à ce que chaque note soit rigoureusement juste sans faire la plus minime concession à la médiocrité.

(2) Au cours de ces exercices *posez* et *maintenez* les doigts bien appuyés sur les cordes partout où la chose est possible.

(3) Observez minutieusement la *valeur* des notes. Veillez y spécialement lorsque deux notes avec coups d'archet *séparés* se trouvent être suivies de deux autres notes de même valeur mais figurant dans un même coup d'archet, ou lorsqu'une note isolée est suivie de trois notes de même valeur dans un même coup d'archet, etc.. Les diverses façons dont les notes peuvent être groupées importent peu, pourvu qu'à chacune d'elles il soit toujours donné sa valeur adéquate.

(4) Commencez par jouer ces exercices *au ralenti* et faites en sorte que les doigts s'élèvent très haut. Il faut vraiment sentir que tout le travail se fait dans les charnières des *articulations*. Abaissez ensuite avec force les doigts sur le manche. Lorsque, par la suite, vous jouez ces exercices en un tempo plus *accéléré*, levez les doigts moins haut et abaissez les sur le manche avec plus de légèreté.

(5) Répartissez vos coups d'archet de manière à jouer d'abord ces exercices en un tempo assez lent mais toujours avec une intonation rigoureusement juste. Dès que vous serez à même de jouer de la sorte avec aisance, accélérez et conformez-vous aux indications des coups d'archet tout en vous appliquant à jouer le plus de notes possibles en un seul coup d'archet.

ZUR BEACHTUNG

(1) Von vordringlicher Wichtigkeit für das Spielen auf Streichinstrumenten ist *untadelig-saubere Intonation*. Diese kann nur erreicht werden durch intensiv-konzentriertes (niemals oberflächliches) *Hören*. Lass keinen Ton durchgehen, der auch nur im geringsten unrein in der Stimmung ist.

(2) Lass bei diesen Übungen die *Finger auf der Saite liegen*, soweit und solange es möglich ist.

(3) Achte auf genaue *Notenwerte*, besonders wenn auf zwei *einzeln gestrichene* Noten unmittelbar zwei *gebundene* Noten gleichen Wertes folgen — oder auf eine einzeln gestrichene Note drei gebundene gleichen Wertes usw. Ganz gleichgültig, wie die Notengruppen auf den Bogen verteilt sind: Stets muss jede Note genau den ihr zugehörigen Wert erhalten.

(4) Beim *langsamen* Üben die Finger hoch (aus dem Knöchelgelenk) aufheben und energisch auf das Griffbrett aufsetzen—beim *schnellen* Üben nur wenig aufheben und locker aufsetzen.

(5) Studiere die Übungen *zuerst langsam* mit sauberer, schöner Tongebung, dann erst halte dich an die angegebenen Bögen oder spiele auf einen Bogen so viel Noten wie möglich.

SEVCIK. Op. 8 – Viola (Alto)

Changement de position

Tâchez que votre intonation reste toujours rigoureusement juste.

Dans tous ces exercices, changements de position sans glissement ou saccades exagérés et veillez à ce que votre jeu soit bien homogène.

En jouant les formules ci-dessous, il faut répéter dans le mouvement modéré:
a) chaque mesure séparément
b) chaque mesure avec la suivante (1-2, 2-3, 3-4 etc.)
c) toutes les mesures, qui sont indiquées sur la même corde (dans le 1er exemple les mesures 1-6, 7-12, 13-18, 19-25)
d) tout l'exemple dans les tons suivants, en lié et en détaché:

Changes of position

Perfect intonation please.

In all these exercises change positions without overdone slides or jerks and play with even tone.

Practise these examples in moderato tempo
a) each bar separately,
b) each bar with the next-following one, thus: 1 to 2, 2 to 3, 3 to 4, etc.
c) all the bars shown to lie on the same string, thus: in the 1st example bars 1 to 6, 7 to 12, 13 to 18, 19 to 25,
d) the whole example in the following keys-both legato and staccato:

Lagenwechselübungen

Untadelige Intonation.

In all diesen Übungen die Lagenwechsel tonlich ganz gleichmässig ohne überflüssigen Rutscher oder Ruck.

Bei dem Einüben dieser Beispiele wiederhole man im gemässigtem Tempo:
a) jeden einzelnen Takt
b) jeden Takt mit dem nächstfolgenden (1-2, 2-3, 3-4 u.s.w.)
c) alle Takte, die auf derselben Saite angezeigt sind (im 1ten Beispiele Takte 1-6, 7-12, 13-18, 19-25)
d) das ganze Beispiel in folgenden Tonarten, gebunden und gestossen:

1

Changement de position:
1-2, 2-3, 3-4 etc.
Jouez cet exercice comme si toutes les notes étaient des doubles croches.

Changes of position:
from 1st to 2nd, 2nd to 3rd, 3rd to 4th etc.
Practise these exercises also as if all notes were semiquavers.

Wechsel der Lagen:
1-2, 2-3, 3-4 u.s.w.
Übe diese Etüde auch in lauter gleichmässigen Sechzehnteln.

2

Surveillez particulièrement votre intonation aux changements de position sur une même note.

Particular attention to intonation when positions change on same note.

Gib besonders Obacht auf die Intonation, wenn der Lagenwechsel auf dem gleichen Ton erfolgt.

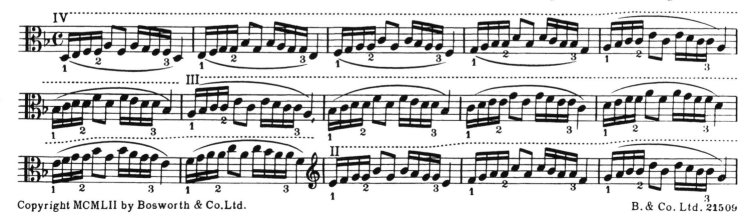

Copyright MCMLII by Bosworth & Co.Ltd.

B. & Co. Ltd. 21509

6

5

Changez de position pour les tons entiers aussi doucement que vous le faites pour les demi-tons.

Change positions as smoothly in the whole tone as you do in the half tone.

Der Lagenwechsel um einen ganzen Ton muss ebenso glatt erfolgen wie beim Wechsel um einen Halbton.

6

7

8

Changement de position: 1-3, 2-4, 3-5 etc.	Changes of position: from 1st to 3rd, 2nd to 4th, 3rd to 5th etc.	Wechsel der Lagen: 1-3, 2-4, 3-5 u.s.w.

9

Pas de heurts. | No jerks. | Ohne jeden Ruck.

10

11

10

12

L'intonation toujours!
Attention aux changements de
position sur une même note.

Intonation!
Great care when you change
position on same note.

Intonation!
Besondre Sorgfalt beim Lagenwechsel auf dem gleichen Ton.

13

B.& Co.Ltd.21509

14

15

16

Changement de position:
1-4, 2-5, 3-6 etc.

Changes of position:
from 1st to 4th, 2nd to 5th,
3rd to 6th, etc.

Wechsel der Lagen:
1-4, 2-5, 3-6 u.s.w.

B. & Co. Ltd. 21509

17

18

19

20

23

Changement de position:
1-5, 2-6, 3-7 etc.

Changes of position:
from 1st to 5th, 2nd to 6th,
3rd to 7th, etc.

Wechsel der Lagen:
1-5, 2-6, 3-7 u.s.w.

24

25

B.&Co.Ltd.21509

29

30

31

B. & Co. Ltd. 21509

32

Changement de position:
1-6, 2-7, 3-8 etc.

Changes of position:
from 1st to 6th, 2nd to 7th,
3rd to 8th, etc.

Wechsel der Lagen:
1-6, 2-7, 3-8 u.s.w.

33

34

35

36

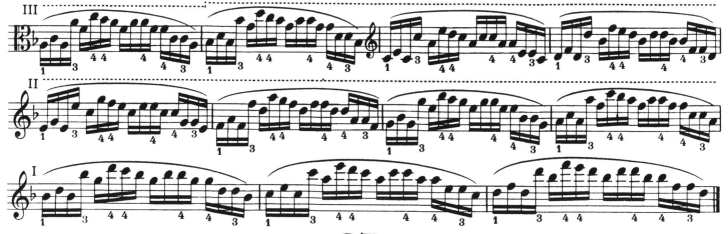

37

B.& Co.Ltd.21509

38

Changement de position:
1-7, 2-8, 3-9 etc.

Changes of position:
from 1st to 7th, 2nd to 8th,
3rd to 9th, etc.

Wechsel der Lagen:
1-7, 2-8, 3-9 u.s.w.

39

40

41

42

43

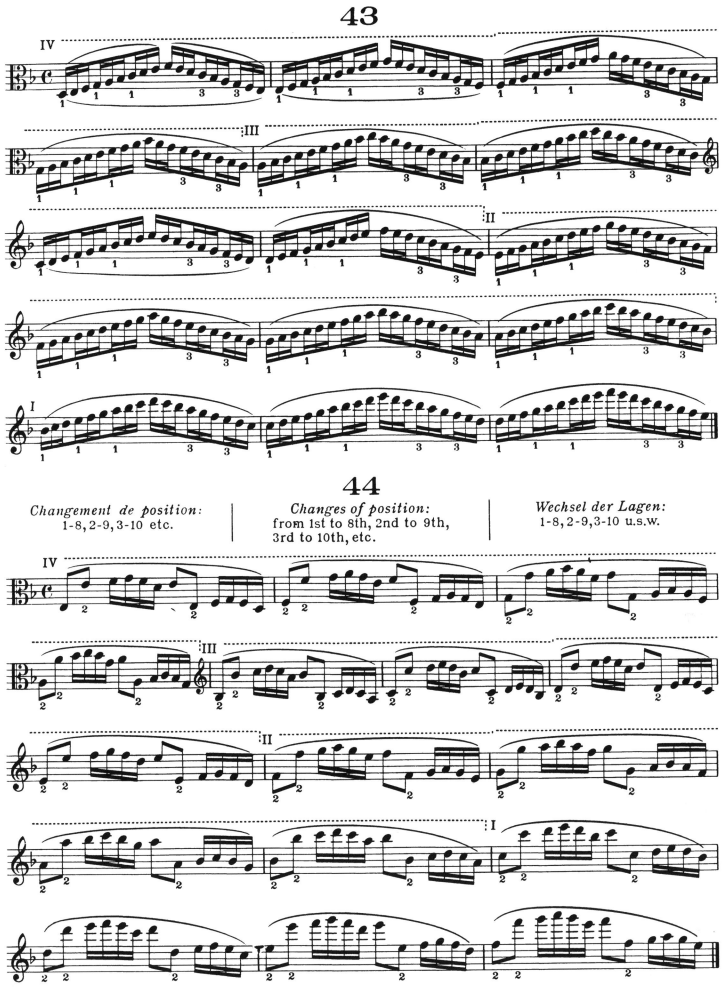

44

| Changement de position: 1-8, 2-9, 3-10 etc. | Changes of position: from 1st to 8th, 2nd to 9th, 3rd to 10th, etc. | Wechsel der Lagen: 1-8, 2-9, 3-10 u.s.w. |

22

45

Gammes de 3 octaves | Scales throughout 3 octaves | Tonleitern durch 3 Oktaven

| On travaillera les Nᵒˢ 45-47 dans tous les tons suivants, en lié et en détaché | Practise Nᵒˢ 45 to 47 in all the following keys both legato and separate bows | Man übe die Nᵒ 45-47 in allen folgenden Tonarten, gebunden und gestossen: |

B. & Co. Ltd. 21509

46

Cet exercice doit également se faire spiccato. | This exercise to be practised spiccato also | Diese Etüde auch spiccato üben!

47

PUBLISHERS OF MUSIC FOR THE SERIOUS VIOLIST

Studies

ARNOLD, Alan
3-Octave Scales & Arpeggios
BLUMENSTENGAL, A.
Viola Scale Technique Bk.1 - 1st Pos.
Viola Scale Technique Bk.2 -1-5 Pos.
HOFMANN, Richard
Melodic Double-Stop Studies Op. 96
TARTINI, Giuseppe
The Art of Bowing

Viola Solo

ARNOLD, Alan
Cadenzas for Telemann Viola Concerto
KREISLER, Fritz
Recitative and Scherzo Caprice
WOEHR, Christian
Bachiana

Viola & Piano Albums

ARNOLD, Alan
The Young Violist Bk. 1 (easy pieces)
The Young Violist Bk. 2 (more pieces)
BACH, J.S.
Basic Bach (arr.Arnold)
BEETHOVEN, Ludwig van
Beethoven's Best (arr. Arnold)
MOZART, W.A
Mozart Miniatures (arr. Arnold)

Viola & Piano Repertoire

BACH, J.S.
Bourrée in C minor
Chromatic Fantasy and Fugue
BEETHOVEN, Ludwig van
Für Elise
BENJAMIN, Arthur
Jamaican Rumba
BOCCHERINI, Luigi
Music Box Minuet
BÖHM, Carl
Sarabande
BOROWSKI, Felix
Adoration
BRAHMS, Johannes
Scherzo
CHOPIN, Frédéric
Nocturne
CORELLI, Arcangelo
Sarabande, Giga and Badinerie
Sonata No.12 - La Folia con Variazione

DANCLA, Charles
Carnival of Venice
DE BÉRIOT, Ch.
Scène de Ballet
DEBUSSY, Claude
Girl with the Flaxen Hair
La Plus Que Lente
DVORÁK, Antonin
Romance Op. 11
Sonatina Op. 100
FAURÉ, Gabriel
Fantasie
FIOCCO, Gioseffo-Hectore
Allegro
FRANCOEUR, François
Sonata in A
GLUCK, Christoff W. von
Melody from *Orfeo ed Euridice*
HANDEL, G.F.
Bourrée
Concerto in B flat
Sonata in B flat
Sonata in D
HUBAY, Jenö
Hejre Kati
JENKINSON, Ezra
Elves' Dance (*Elfentanz*)
JOPLIN, Scott
Pineapple Rag
Solace
KREISLER, Fritz
Liebesfreud
Liebesleid
Praeludium and Allegro
Sicilienne and Rigaudon
MASSENET, Jules
Meditation from *Thaïs*
MATTHEWS, Holon
Fantasy
MENDELSSOHN, Felix
Sonata in E flat
MOZART, W.A.
Adagio K.261
Menuetto Divertimento K.334
Rondo K.250
Serenata Cantabile
MUSSORGSKY, Modest
Hopak
NOVACEK, Ottokar
Perpetual Motion
PAGANINI, Niccolò
Six Sonatas Bk. 1, Nos 1, 2,3
Six Sonatas Bk. 2, Nos 4, 5, 6
Variations on the G-String
PUGNANI, Gaetano
Gavotta Variata

RACHMANINOFF, Sergei
Vocalise
RIES, Franz
Perpetuum Mobile
RIMSKY-KORSAKOV, N.
Flight of the Bumble Bee
SCHMIDT, Ernst
Alla Turca
SHUBERT, Franz
The Bee
TARTINI, Giuseppe
Sonata angelique
The Devil's Trill
TCHAIKOVSKY, P.
Canzonetta
June Barcarolle
Mélodie
Sérénade mélancholique
Valse sentimentale
VITALI, Giovanni
Chaconne
VIVALDI, Antonio
Sonata in G
WEBER, Carl M.
Andante and Hungarian Rondo
WIENIAWSKI, Henryk
Légende
Scherzo Tarantella

Viola Duos

BACH, J. S.
Fifteen Two-Part Inventions
MOZART, W.A.
Duo Sonata in B flat K.292
Twelve Duets K.487

3 Violas & Piano

PACHELBEL, Johann
Canon

4 Violas

TELEMANN, Georg Philipp
Concerto No. 1 in C for 4 Violas
Concerto No. 2 in G for 4 Violas
Concerto No. 3 in F for 4 Violas
Concerto No. 4 in D for 4 Violas

4 Violas & Piano

VIVALDI, Antonio
Concerto for 4 Violas and Piano

Available from:

Bosworth